PENGUIN BOOKS

FIGHT OLIGARCHY

Bernie Sanders is the longest-serving Independent member of Congress in American history. As Chairman of the Budget Committee, he helped write the $1.9 trillion American Rescue Plan, one of the most significant pieces of US legislation in modern times. An inspiring leader in the fight against economic inequality and corporate influence in government, his wildly popular Fighting Oligarchy tour is proving inspirational to millions of Americans across the US. His books include *It's OK to be Angry about Capitalism*, a Sunday Times bestseller.

BERNIE SANDERS

Fight Oligarchy
Where We Go from Here

PENGUIN BOOKS

PENGUIN BOOKS

UK | USA | Canada | Ireland | Australia
India | New Zealand | South Africa

Penguin Books is part of the Penguin Random House group of companies whose addresses can be found at global.penguinrandomhouse.com.

Penguin Random House UK
One Embassy Gardens, 8 Viaduct Gardens, London SW11 7BW

penguin.co.uk

First published in the USA by Crown Publishing Group 2025
First published in Great Britain in Penguin Books 2025
001

Copyright © Bernie Sanders, 2025

The moral right of the author has been asserted

Penguin Random House values and supports copyright.
Copyright fuels creativity, encourages diverse voices, promotes freedom of expression and supports a vibrant culture. Thank you for purchasing an authorized edition of this book and for respecting intellectual property laws by not reproducing, scanning or distributing any part of it by any means without permission. You are supporting authors and enabling Penguin Random House to continue to publish books for everyone.
No part of this book may be used or reproduced in any manner for the purpose of training artificial intelligence technologies or systems. In accordance with Article 4(3) of the DSM Directive 2019/790, Penguin Random House expressly reserves this work from the text and data mining exception.

Printed and bound in Great Britain by Clays Ltd, Elcograf S.p.A.

The authorized representative in the EEA is Penguin Random House Ireland, Morrison Chambers, 32 Nassau Street, Dublin D02 YH68

A CIP catalogue record for this book is available from the British Library

ISBN: 978-1-837-31294-8

Penguin Random House is committed to a sustainable future for our business, our readers and our planet. This book is made from Forest Stewardship Council® certified paper.

*This book is dedicated to my grandchildren
Dylan, Tess, Ella, and Cole.
Like all young people on this planet, they deserve the
right to live in a world of peace, democracy, justice,
and environmental sanity. Let's make it happen.*

CONTENTS

Prologue 1

1 What Is Oligarchy? 3

2 Trump, Oligarchy, and Authoritarianism ... 19

3 Global Oligarchy: Billionaires Win, the World Suffers 51

4 They Did It Then, We Can Do It Now: Some Lessons from History 69

5 Fighting Oligarchy 87

6 Where Do We Go from Here? 105

FIGHT OLIGARCHY

PROLOGUE

I launched the Fighting Oligarchy tour in January 2025. Right away, I was amazed at the passionate response. People across the country, from both red and blue states, came out in huge numbers that I had never seen before. They were there to join the fight against Trump and the oligarchs, and take back control of our government and our country.

Some pundits and politicians have argued that the term "oligarchy" isn't something that ordinary people understand. I disagree. The overwhelming majority of Americans instinctively know, based on their daily struggles, that we live in a country today of extreme inequality—and that our economy and politics have been stolen by the billionaire class.

Understanding how we got here, and how we can change things for the better, is the goal of this book.

1

WHAT IS OLIGARCHY?

Oligarchy is a system in which a small number of extremely wealthy individuals control the economic, political, and media life of a nation. It is a system in which ordinary people have very little power to determine the future of their country. If you're an American, it is the system in which you're living. Increasingly, it is the system that is dominating people in almost every country on Earth.

In America today, we have more income and wealth inequality than we have ever had in the history of our country. Right now, the people on top have never had it so good. Meanwhile, while the rich get richer, the middle class struggles to pay the rent, put food on the table, and pay for health care. The poor live in desperation. Today, one man—Elon Musk—now owns more wealth than the bottom 52 percent of American households. Let me repeat that. One man, worth nearly $400 billion, now owns more wealth than the bottom 52 percent of American households. The top 1 percent own more wealth than the bottom 93 percent. And the CEOs of large corporations make 350 times more than their average employee.

But it's not just income and wealth inequality that make this an oligarchy. In America today, we have more concentration of ownership than we have ever had, with a small number of giant corporations controlling sector after sector of our economy.

Do you want to know why the prices of beef, pork, and chicken are so high in our nation's grocery stores? Well, maybe it has something to do with the fact that just four companies in America control 80 percent of the processing of beef, 70 percent of pork, and nearly 60 percent of poultry.

And it's not just agriculture. The same is true for transportation, financial services, energy, health care, Big Tech—you name it. In America today, a handful of multinational corporations determine what is produced, how employees are treated, and the prices we pay.

And who owns these multinational corporations?

Well, if you can believe it, three huge Wall Street firms. Vanguard, BlackRock, and State Street are the major stockholders in 95 percent of S&P 500 corporations. In other words, they have significant influence over many hundreds of companies that employ millions of American workers—and, in fact, the entire economy.

You want to know who owns General Motors? Well, their three largest shareholders are Vanguard, BlackRock, and State Street.

Okay. But who owns Ford, GM's supposed

rival? If you guessed Vanguard, BlackRock, and State Street, in that same exact order, you would be correct.

What about the big oil companies, ExxonMobil and Chevron? That's right. Vanguard, BlackRock, and State Street are the three largest shareholders of both those companies.

How about Pfizer, Merck, and Johnson & Johnson, three huge pharmaceutical companies? Yup. Vanguard, BlackRock, and State Street own all three.

Over the last several years, both as chairman and ranking member of the Health, Education, Labor and Pensions (HELP) Committee in the Senate, I have advocated on behalf of union workers who were engaged in labor struggles against a number of corporations for better wages, benefits, and working conditions. And time and time again, when I contacted the managers of these companies, I was told, in so many words: "We're not the owners, it's somebody else."

That opaque consolidation of power makes

it harder to hold ownership accountable for their actions.

The media, which is supposed to objectively inform us as to what is happening in our country and the world, is now also controlled by a handful of giant international conglomerates and billionaires. That's why issues that impact the working class of this country, or serious analyses of wealth and power, get relatively little airtime. That's why there has never been a TV program focused on why the United States, alone among wealthy countries, does not guarantee health care for all or provide guaranteed paid family and medical leave. That's why we hear virtually nothing about the growing gap between the rich and the poor. Topics like these are just not of great interest to the billionaires who own the networks.

In America today, we have more media concentration than we have ever had. Just six international media corporations control what 90 percent of the American people see, hear, and read. They own the traditional media—newspapers, radio and TV networks, movie studios—as well as much of the internet.

Elon Musk, the wealthiest man on Earth, owns X (formerly Twitter); Jeff Bezos, the fourth wealthiest person in the world, owns *The Washington Post*, Amazon Prime, and the streaming platform Twitch; and Mark Zuckerberg, who is now the third wealthiest man alive, owns Meta, which controls Instagram, Facebook, and WhatsApp. Larry Ellison, the second wealthiest man on Earth, just purchased Paramount, which owns CBS. Rupert Murdoch, another multibillionaire, owns Fox, *The Wall Street Journal*, the *New York Post*, HarperCollins, and right-wing media throughout the world. Billionaires own and control virtually every major newspaper and radio network in the country.

Oligarchy today has not only produced unprecedented income and wealth inequality. It has not only created an unprecedented concentration of ownership. It has also given us an extremely corrupt political system that is heavily dominated by billionaires and their super PACs. Increasingly, American elections are not about candidates and ideas. They are about the competing ads that billionaire-controlled super PACs produce.

In 2010, the U.S. Supreme Court ruled 5–4 in the *Citizens United* case that billionaires could spend as much as they want on political campaigns. And that's what they're doing. Since that decision was made, political spending on elections has gone up by more than 1,600 percent. In the 2024 election, 100 billionaire families spent $2.6 billion—double what they spent in 2020.

Elon Musk alone spent $290 million to elect Trump. His reward: He became the most powerful person in government and was able to establish the Department of Government Efficiency (DOGE), where he was allowed to implement his extreme right-wing ideology by dismantling federal agencies and throwing tens of thousands of federal employees out on the street.

But the impact of a corrupt campaign finance

system goes beyond presidential campaigns. It goes right to the heart of the legislative process in Washington.

In early July 2025, Republicans in Congress passed Trump's "Big Beautiful Bill"—the most destructive piece of legislation in modern American history. While providing $1 trillion in tax breaks to the top 1 percent, this bill makes massive cuts to Medicaid, nutrition, and education.

Almost every Republican member of the House and the Senate voted for this horrific bill. Why? Do you think they didn't know about the impact that these enormous cuts to Medicaid and the Affordable Care Act would have on their constituents—many of whom are working-class and poor? They knew. But what they also knew was that if they voted against that legislation, on the very next day oligarchs with unlimited resources would announce that their super PACs would be running a candidate against them in the next election. And the likely result is they would lose.

That is exactly what happened to Senator Thom

Tillis of North Carolina. Tillis announced his opposition to this terrible bill because it would cause over 650,000 people in his state to lose their health insurance. The next day, Trump ruthlessly denounced him and threatened to primary him. A few hours later, Tillis issued a statement saying that he would not seek reelection. The oligarchs do not take no for an answer. They expect the candidates they fund to follow orders and do as they are told.

But it was not just the "Big Beautiful Bill" that catered to the needs of wealthy campaign contributors. In December 2024, after months of difficult negotiations, the Senate and the House announced that they had reached a bipartisan agreement on a major appropriations bill. As chairman of the HELP Committee, I was heavily involved in those negotiations and worked hard to put funding into that package to expand primary health care, dental care, mental health care, nutrition programs for the elderly, and apprenticeship programs for young adults. Was this bipartisan agreement everything that I wanted? No. Not by a long shot. But it was a lot better than nothing and would, in fact, provide help to millions of struggling Americans.

Just as Congress was set to pass that appropriations bill, it was torpedoed by a series of tweets from Elon Musk, who, among other things, pledged to primary anyone who dared to vote for that legislation. And just like that, months of painstaking negotiations went down the tubes. Musk spoke. The bill died. Millions of Americans will suffer as a result.

But it's not just Republicans who are under the influence of billionaire money. Oligarchs have enormous power over the Democratic Party as well. A few recent examples:

While outspent by Republican billionaires, over eighty Democratic billionaires donated hundreds of millions trying to elect Kamala Harris president in the 2024 election. In my view, their heavy influence on her campaign cost her an election that should have been won. Instead of running a campaign that took on powerful special interests, and making it clear that she would fight for the working class of our country, she ran a campaign designed not to antagonize the business community and the oligarchs. In fact, one of her main spokespersons was the billionaire Mark Cuban.

Billionaire influence on Democrats goes well beyond campaigns. It impacts decision-making on some of the most significant moral and foreign policy issues that we face. On October 7, 2023, Hamas, a terrorist organization, carried out a horrific attack against Israel that killed 1,200 innocent people and took over 250 hostages. Israel, like any country that suffered such an attack, had a right to defend itself. But Israel did not have the right to wage an all-out war against the Palestinian people, as it has done in clear violation of international law.

That war, as of this writing, has resulted in the deaths of some 60,000 people and the wounding of over 146,000—in a population of only 2.2 million people in Gaza. Most of the victims have been women, children, and the elderly. The UN reports that at least 18,500 children have been killed, 12,000 of whom were twelve years old or younger.

This is in addition to the 25,000 who were injured. More than 3,000 children in Gaza have had one or more limbs amputated. As a result of the blocking of humanitarian aid, international aid organizations have determined that widespread malnutrition is taking place, and many cases of starvation have been reported. Starving Palestinians have been shot down in cold blood as they gathered at food distribution centers. Further, the entire infrastructure of Gaza—housing, the health care system, schools, water, and wastewater plants—has been almost completely destroyed.

Do you think that Democrats and Republicans in Congress aren't aware of what's going on in Gaza? Do you doubt that many of them are disgusted with the behavior of Netanyahu and how Israel is waging this barbaric war? Of course they are. Why, then, do they continue to vote for billions of U.S. dollars to support this war? The answer is that many of them understand that if they vote against military aid for Israel, they will face strong opposition from the American Israel Public Affairs Committee (AIPAC). And that's not an idle threat. AIPAC spent $100 million in 2024 to oppose and defeat members of Congress, like Cori Bush in Missouri and Jamaal Bowman in New York, who had the courage to oppose U.S. aid for the Netanyahu government.

In other words, key components of American foreign policy are now determined by super PACs and the billionaires who fund them.

But this political corruption is not just limited to what goes on in our nation's capital. It now takes place in virtually every state and large city in America.

Here's just one particularly obscene example: After Zohran Mamdani defeated the Establishment candidate, former governor Andrew Cuomo, in the Democratic primary for mayor of New York City, the oligarchs panicked. Wall Street and real estate speculators would not accept that a pro-working-class candidate won the primary. Quite openly, on the front pages of New York newspapers, billionaires announced that they would spend hundreds of millions of dollars to defeat him.

Oligarchy impacts not only our economic and political life, but our culture as well. Corporate greed and the never-ending search for more and more profits largely determine the movies that we see, the music that we hear, and what our kids consider to be "cool."

As a young person in Brooklyn, I grew up with the Brooklyn Dodgers. I, and millions of others, will never forget how that team was yanked out of Brooklyn and moved to Los Angeles by a greedy owner. The situation today is far worse. I find it remarkable how oligarchy now has control over virtually every professional baseball, basketball, football, or hockey team that Americans root for. Today, almost every professional sports team is owned by a billionaire family, a conglomerate, or a Wall Street investment firm.

One example out of many: The Los Angeles Lakers were recently purchased by Mark Walter, the CEO and chairman of TWG Global, a multinational conglomerate. He is also the major owner of the Los Angeles Dodgers. In other words, one man now controls the two major sports teams in the second largest city in America. The result of billionaire control of professional sports is that it is increasingly difficult, if not impossible, for working-class families to afford to go see their favorite teams play ball.

For years now, the power of the oligarchs has grown, putting democracy on the defensive. And then, in the midst of all this, Donald Trump wins the presidential election.

2

TRUMP, OLIGARCHY, AND AUTHORITARIANISM

Trump was inaugurated on January 20, 2025. I had the misfortune of sitting in the front row to witness the spectacle. As many will recall, right behind Trump as he took the oath of office were the three wealthiest men in America—Elon Musk, Jeff Bezos, and Mark Zuckerberg. And right behind them were thirteen other billionaires whom Trump had nominated to head up major federal agencies.

As I listened to Trump's terrible speech, I was remembering my American history. In 1863, a few days after the Battle of Gettysburg, where thousands of soldiers died fighting to end the abomination of slavery, Abraham Lincoln told the American people that "these dead shall not have died in vain, that this nation, under God, shall have a new birth of freedom, and that government of the people, by the people, for the people, shall not perish from the earth."

Well. At Trump's inauguration I was witnessing, up front, a very different vision of government. It was a government of the billionaire class, by the billionaire class, for the billionaire class. Not a pleasant sight.

Trumpism is about many things, but at its core its goals are no different than what demagogues have always sought—wealth and power.

Under Trump, unless we stop him, the very rich will become much richer and more powerful while working families will fall further and further behind. Trump, unless we stop him, will gather more and more power into his own hands, undermine the rule of law and our democracy, and move us rapidly toward an authoritarian society.

And Trump and his acolytes are not wasting any time. They are aggressively moving forward. In his "Big Beautiful Bill," passed in early July 2025, the 1 percent received over a trillion dollars in tax breaks, including a $211 billion estate-tax break for the top two-tenths of the 1 percent who stand to inherit over $30 million. In that same bill, the large corporations that they own received over $900 billion in tax breaks. This bill amounted to the largest transfer of wealth in modern American history.

But that's not all. Trump, on behalf of his fellow oligarchs, has also pursued a very strong anti-union agenda. The National Labor Relations Board (NLRB), which was created to protect union rights, has been effectively shut down—making it harder for workers to organize. Several major federal trade unions, representing over a million workers, have been illegally broken. By firing tens of thousands of federal employees, Trump has given a green light to corporate CEOs, letting them know that workers' rights do not have to be respected.

Further, through his outrageous lies about waste

and fraud in Social Security and other federal programs, Trump is laying the groundwork for massive privatization efforts in the future. Or, as Elon Musk said, the goal is for the U.S. government to privatize "as much as possible." The opportunity to make billions by taking over federal and state programs like Social Security, Medicare, Medicaid, public education, NASA, and public transportation is just what the oligarchs have dreamed about for years.

Under Trump, some of the very wealthiest oligarchs have gotten special deals. Jeff Bezos used his support for Trump to accompany him to Saudi Arabia and obtain a $5 billion contract from Mohammed bin Salman (MBS), the repressive ruler of Saudi Arabia, to create an Artificial Intelligence Zone in his country designed by Amazon Web Services. Ironically, this is the same MBS who ordered the brutal murder of Jamal Khashoggi, a columnist for *The Washington Post*, owned by Bezos. What a great example of oligarch loyalty.

And then there is Mark Zuckerberg. Not only

did Zuckerberg contribute $1 million to Trump's inauguration fund (along with Musk and Bezos), he also gave $25 million to Trump to settle his frivolous lawsuit against Meta and Instagram. And Zuckerberg's bribes are beginning to pay off. Trump's "Big Beautiful Bill" contains a $15 billion retroactive tax break for Meta.

Under Trumpism, where uncontrolled greed is a driving force, it's not just the oligarchs around him who have benefited. In an extraordinary and unprecedented level of kleptocracy, Trump and his family have made billions off of his position as president. Trump raised a record $239 million for his presidential inauguration committee. To curry favor with the Trump administration, many companies and individuals donated to the committee, including Amazon, Meta, Uber, and Google—each ponying up $1 million. The CEOs of OpenAI and Apple each personally donated the same amount.

Trump has accepted a $400 million luxury jet from the government of Qatar for his personal use, and has established his own crypto coin, which has made him $1.2 billion richer—and counting. Donald Trump Jr., alongside tech billionaires, launched an invite-only club in Washington, D.C., that costs more than $500,000 to join.

Family members have developed extremely beneficial business relationships with foreign governments. His son-in-law Jared Kushner received a $2 billion investment from Saudi Arabia for his private equity firm, despite failing to return any profits. And the governments of Qatar, the United Arab Emirates, and Saudi Arabia have all made lucrative real estate deals with the Trump Organization—including golf courses, resorts, and events. It's no surprise that the first foreign trip of Trump's second term was to—you guessed it—Saudi Arabia, Qatar, and the UAE, where he was joined by Elon Musk, OpenAI CEO Sam Altman, and other tech oligarchs.

How Trumpism Evolved

To understand Trumpism, how it functions and how it can be defeated, it's important to understand the conditions that allowed Trump to come to power, and how he is utilizing that power.

For years now I have been asked the same questions over and over again: How could the American people support a crooked businessman involved in over four thousand lawsuits, a pathological liar, racist, sexist, xenophobe, bully, and convicted felon? How could working-class Americans vote in large numbers for someone who supports massive tax breaks for the rich and drastic cuts in federal programs that low-income and working people desperately need?

And I answer those questions, over and over again, by stating that Trump's rise to power has everything to do with the reality that, over the last many decades, the Democratic Party has turned its back on the needs and suffering of America's working class. While party leaders hustled campaign contributions from the rich and the powerful, millions of working families throughout the country fell into despair and political isolation. Donald Trump filled the political vacuum that the Democrats created.

Trump, unlike most Democrats, campaigned with the understanding that the current economic system is broken and failing the vast majority of Americans. He understood that the United States consists of more than well-educated, upper-middle-class people on the East and West Coasts. He understood that more and more people were getting their information from the internet and not CNN or MSNBC. He understood that tens of millions of Americans feel betrayed politically, are increasingly distrustful of all major institutions, are disgusted with the status quo, and desperately want change. Pathetically, while state Democratic parties were collapsing throughout rural America, this billionaire phony became the agent of that change.

Let's understand what the Democratic Party

leadership does not care to understand. In America today, there is an enormous amount of pain. There is anger. There is frustration. There is fear. There is disappointment. People vote every two years or every four years. Candidates make promises. Nothing happens. Life does not get better. It often gets worse.

The working class of this country see, in their daily existence, that the economic system in which they live is rigged, designed to benefit the very rich and powerful, while they fall further and further behind. They are hurting—badly.

Despite an explosion of technology over the last fifty years, and a huge increase in worker productivity, the average American worker today is making less each week than he or she did in 1973, after adjusting for inflation. Meanwhile, the billionaire class has never had it so good. During that same fifty-year period, there was, according to the RAND Corporation, a $79 trillion transfer of wealth from the bottom 90 percent to the top 1 percent.

As a result of disastrous trade agreements like the North American Free Trade Agreement (NAFTA) and Permanent Normal Trade Relations (PNTR) with China, tens of thousands of American factories were shut down and millions of decent-paying jobs were sent to low-wage countries. Once-vibrant middle-class communities throughout our country were hollowed out and their inhabitants driven into poverty. That betrayal of the working class by the political establishment has not been forgotten.

In the United States, at this moment, 60 percent of Americans live paycheck to paycheck as they try to put food on the table, pay the rent, or afford medical care. Think about that for a moment. While it is virtually ignored in the corporate media and not meaningfully discussed by either major political party, in the wealthiest country on Earth a majority of people are struggling to survive every single day.

Nearly half of all older workers in our country have no retirement savings and face living out their "golden" years on inadequate Social Security benefits—which some Republicans are threatening to cut. Over 20 percent of senior citizens are trying to survive on less than $15,000 a year, and are forced to deplete what meager savings they may have if they utilize Medicaid for their nursing home care.

We have the highest rate of childhood poverty of almost any major country on Earth, our childcare system is dysfunctional, and millions of kids are dependent on school lunch programs for the one decent meal they receive per day. Have you ever spoken to a single mom trying to raise kids on fifteen dollars an hour? I have. Not a pleasant discussion.

As a result of our national housing crisis, nearly 800,000 Americans are homeless and over 20 million households spend half or more of their limited income on housing. How can you afford to buy your kid decent food when half your paycheck goes for housing? Where do you move when your landlord raises your rent by 20 percent and you can't afford to pay it? What happens to your child when he or she has to change schools because you're forced to move? Those are questions that too many Americans are now trying to answer.

We remain the only major country on Earth that does not guarantee health care to all as a human right. The result: 85 million are uninsured or underinsured, we pay the highest prices in the world for prescription drugs, and over 60,000 Americans die each year because they can't get to a doctor on time. Unbelievably, 42 percent of cancer patients deplete their entire life savings within the first two years of their diagnosis. And with Trump's "Big Beautiful Bill," the situation will get much worse. How can you live a normal life if you have to worry about whether you can pay the medical bills when you or someone in your family gets sick?

Add it all up: low wages, inadequate health insurance, retirement insecurity, unaffordable housing, and healthy food that is too expensive, and you can understand why, all across the country, working people want structural changes to a broken economic and political system. The status quo is not working for them. And on top of all that, parents worry that their kids will be even worse off than they are.

And that desperation is sometimes fatal. I will never forget a hearing I held in the Senate some years ago where physicians discussed what they called "diseases of despair." They described the patients they treated whose lives were cut short because of the unbearable stress they experienced—people who succumbed to drugs, alcohol, tobacco, obesity, or suicide because they had essentially given up hope for a better life. Today in America, at a time when we as a nation have one of the shortest life expectancies of any major country, the bottom 50 percent of our society live, on average, seven fewer years than the top 1 percent.

That is where we are today. And, you ask me, where have the Democrats been?

That's why Donald Trump is president.

Trump: Just One More Demagogue

But let's be honest. Trump did more than just seize upon the economic anxieties that millions of working-class people experience, and the failure of the Democratic Party to address them. He did what demagogues, cowards, and authoritarians have always done. Instead of trying to find real solutions to the very serious crises facing our country, and helping us understand the causes of these problems, he scapegoats powerless minorities and, with ugly, vicious, and dishonest rhetoric, blames them for society's problems. For political gain, he turns one group of people against another. He creates fear, lots of fear. It is always us against them. Whites versus Blacks. Native-born versus immigrants. Heterosexuals versus gay and transgender people. Christians versus Muslims. Americans versus the rest of the world.

Sadly, fear and hatred are very powerful emotions, and Trump effectively uses them to his advantage. It's true in the United States, as it is all over the world. Racism, sexism, xenophobia, and homophobia can win votes.

For Trump, creating hatred, fear, and divisiveness is nothing new. That's what his politics has always been about. In 1989, amid crime problems in New York City and after a white woman was raped and beaten in Central Park while she was jogging, Trump ran full-page ads in New York newspapers demanding the death penalty for the five Black and Latino teenagers who were arrested for the crime. His ad talked about a "world ruled by the law of the streets as roving bands of wild criminals roam our neighborhoods." As it happened, the young men arrested turned out to be innocent, and years later they were released from prison.

When Barack Obama was president, Trump amplified the conspiracy theory that Obama was born in Kenya, not the United States, and was an illegitimate president. In doing so, he not only undermined the credibility of the Democratic president of the United States, he also stoked racism against our first Black president and xenophobia against a man whose father was born a Muslim in Africa.

The pattern, from then to now, remains the same. Deflect attention away from the causes and solutions of the major crises facing society by creating fear and uncertainty, blaming an "other," and proposing and implementing harsh remedies. *No. We can't get you decent wages, affordable housing, or health care as a human right—but we will certainly make the "others" suffer.* Your satisfaction comes not from an improvement in your quality of life, but by making others' lives worse.

And all of this is amplified by Trump's use of the Big Lie.

Now, you're not going to be shocked when I tell you that many politicians lie. Nothing new there. But what I will tell you is that Trump, a pathological liar, has introduced a whole new level of dishonesty and deceit into the political process. Sometimes I am not sure that even he knows the difference between a lie and the truth. Perhaps he simply says whatever pops into his mouth. But, most often, his lies are calculated. And the impact is profound and extremely destructive.

When Trump claims that he won the 2020 election, he is undermining American democracy and the integrity of our entire political system. Why bother to vote or even have elections if the results can't be trusted?

When Trump claims that the insurrection of January 6, 2021, when 140 police officers were injured while defending the Capitol from his supporters, was a "day of love"—and then pardons the rioters—he is condoning violence as a political tool. Why accept election results if you can forcibly overturn them? Why accept the rule of law? Might makes right.

When Trump claims that climate change is a "hoax" emanating from China, he is not only undermining faith in science and the overwhelming majority of researchers—who believe the warming of the planet is caused by human activity—he is also making it far more difficult to address this existential threat. Why put resources into transforming our energy system away from fossil fuel if climate change is not caused by carbon emissions?

When Trump claims that criticism of him by the mainstream media is "fake news," who can we trust to tell us what's going on in the world? If the journalists at ABC, CBS, NBC, CNN, PBS, NPR, *The New York Times*, *The Wall Street Journal*, and other mainstream media are all lying, why should we listen to them? Is Fox the only reliable news outlet, or is it only Donald Trump or some conspiracy theorist on the internet who will tell us the truth?

Trump's Big Lies are enormously effective in undermining the democratic political process, especially when they are pushed out to millions through right-wing internet outlets. They also make it easier for others to follow in his footsteps. *If the president of the United States can tell outrageous lies, why can't I? Who cares? Is "truth" anything more than what I say it is, repeated over and over again?*

Further, it is not an accident that Trump has hired a host of articulate former Fox TV communicators to run major federal agencies. Trump and his team are relentlessly out there, every day, pushing their (often blatantly) dishonest perspectives. They are out in the mainstream media. They are out on Fox News and other right-wing outlets. They are on podcasts. They are all over the internet. No administration has ever been as aggressive in pushing their agenda in the media. No administration has ever understood the effectiveness of constant, round-the-clock communication.

Trumpism, in all its ugliness, was on full display on March 4, 2025, when the president gave his State of the Union address before a joint session of Congress. As a senator from Vermont, I was there. Some 36 million watched on TV. And it was a night to remember. The Big Lies. The fearmongering. The hatred. The racism. The homophobia. He laid it all out. A disturbing and unforgettable show.

Trump spoke for about 100 minutes and, in his remarks, managed to ignore almost every major problem facing our country. Not a word about income and wealth inequality, or the economic plight of millions of working-class Americans. Not a word about a corrupt campaign finance system. Not a word about our broken and wildly expensive health care system. Not a word about the housing crisis. Not a word about the high cost of prescription drugs. And most certainly no reference to the existential threat of climate change.

What did he talk about for an hour and forty minutes? Well. He spent a considerable amount of time throwing out blatant lies about the Social Security system. According to Trump, there was massive fraud in the system and "millions and millions" of Social Security checks were going out to people over the age of 140—even to people who were over 200 years old. Wow! Incredible!

Needless to say, it was all a lie. A short time later, I attended a hearing where Trump's own nominee to lead the Social Security Administration acknowledged that well over 99 percent of Social Security checks were going out to people who earned those benefits. No one who was 150 or 200 or 300 years old was receiving Social Security benefits.

Why did Trump present such blatant falsehoods about Social Security? Not hard to understand. This was part of a very calculated effort to undermine faith in government, give himself more power, and open the way for massive privatization. If you could convince the American people that the government was so broken and ineffective that it was unable to even administer Social Security, what could government do? It was not an accident that, only a few days before Trump's speech, Elon Musk stated that Social Security is "the biggest Ponzi scheme of all time." Another total lie.

Social Security is the most popular federal program in our country's history, and has been in effect since 1935. During that time, it has never once failed to provide benefits to those who have earned them. Last year, it kept over 27 million Americans out of poverty. Some Ponzi scheme! Trump's lies took place at the same time as Elon Musk and his DOGE folks were laying off many thousands of civil servants in the Social Security Administration.

During his speech, Trump also spent considerable time discussing how transgender athletes are impacting women's sports. He even introduced, from the House balcony, a young woman who was allegedly injured in a volleyball game by a transgender athlete. Eighty-five million Americans are uninsured or underinsured and can't afford health care? No mention. An injury on a volleyball court? Lengthy discussion.

But, according to Trump, it was not just transgender athletes that we have to fear. An even greater threat to our country is undocumented immigrants.

Now, few will deny that immigration is a difficult and controversial issue. That's not new. That has been the case throughout the history of our country.

In 1882, the U.S. Congress passed the Chinese Exclusion Act, which prohibited the immigration of Chinese laborers because of economic tensions. That act was not repealed until 1943.

The 1924 Immigration Act dramatically reduced immigration and established country by country quotas. This greatly reduced the number of immigrants from southern and eastern Europe. It also effectively excluded Asians from becoming American citizens.

The Immigration and Nationality Act of 1965 opened the doors to "those who can contribute most to this country—to its growth, to its strength, to its spirit." The new law created a preference system that focused on immigrants' skills and family relations with citizens or U.S. residents. It also, for the first time, set a visa quota for the Western Hemisphere of 120,000 per year.

In recent times, as a result of poverty, harmful trade policies, drug cartel violence, and climate change, millions of people from Central America and Latin America have left their homes and, often with young children, made the long and dangerous trek to the border, where they illegally entered the United States. Today, there are about 11 million undocumented immigrants in our country, approximately 3 percent of our population.

Why did they come here? They came here

for exactly the same reason that millions of immigrants—including my father, who came from Poland—have always come to the United States. They came to flee poverty and in search of a better life for themselves and their kids.

Is sneaking across the border a violation of U.S. law? Of course it is. Should we have stronger border security? Yes. Should undocumented people who commit serious crimes be deported? Yes. Is the United States immigration system broken? Yes. Should Congress, after years of debate, finally pass comprehensive immigration reform? Yes.

There is widespread agreement on all of that.

But where there are differences of opinion, strong differences, is in how we respond to people who break the law—including undocumented immigrants. And this is an area where Donald Trump's approach has been extremely racist, selective, and frankly, disgusting and self-serving.

If you are a violent insurrectionist who attempted to undermine American democracy, and who injured law enforcement officers protecting the nation's Capitol: No problem. You broke the law but you get pardoned.

If you are a wealthy businessman convicted of tax evasion and your family makes a million-dollar contribution to the president's super PAC: No problem. You broke the law but you get pardoned.

If you are a sheriff who was a strong political supporter of Trump and you get convicted of bribery: No problem. You broke the law but you get pardoned.

If you are a former Trump campaign chairman convicted of bank and tax fraud: No problem. You broke the law but you get pardoned.

If your son is married to the president's daughter and you were convicted of tax evasion and witness tampering and served two years in jail: No problem. You broke the law but you get pardoned. (In addition, you get appointed to be ambassador to France.)

But if you are an impoverished, undocumented immigrant who entered this country illegally, that's a very different story. Despite the fact that you may be working hard and raising a family, you are verbally attacked in the most hateful ways imaginable. You are described as less than human. No compassion here. No pardons here.

When Trump first announced his intention to run for president in 2015, he made the focus of his remarks an attack on Mexican migrants: "They're bringing drugs. They're bringing crime. They're rapists." That's how he described our neighbors to the south. And it's been downhill from there.

Just last year, during the 2024 presidential debate, Trump made outrageous accusations that Haitian Americans were stealing and eating people's pets in Springfield, Ohio. During that campaign, he also echoed Nazi language by stating that migrants were invading the United States and that "illegal immigration is poisoning the blood of our nation. They're coming from prisons, from mental institutions—from all over the world."

And his hateful rhetoric and the demonizing of the undocumented didn't stop after he won the election. It continued right into his State of the

Union speech. In describing Mexico during that speech, he stated: "The territory to the immediate south of our border is now dominated entirely by criminal cartels that murder, rape, torture, and exercise total control—they have total control over a whole Nation—posing a grave threat to our national security."

On two occasions during his remarks he felt it necessary to describe, in great detail, horrible crimes committed by murderers who were undocumented. In describing the terrible murder of Laken Riley, a twenty-two-year-old nursing student, he mentioned how she had been "viciously attacked, assaulted, beaten, brutalized, and horrifically murdered." In detailing the horrible murder of a twelve-year-old girl from Texas, he stated that "she was kidnapped, tied up, assaulted for two hours under a bridge, and horrifically murdered."

The goal here for Trump is not difficult to understand. Through inflammatory rhetoric, not dissimilar from that used by demagogues around the world, Trump is attempting to convey the image that the undocumented people in this country are savages. They are murderers. They are dangerous. They are our enemies. We must fear them. We must hate them. We must get rid of them. There is no priority more important than that. Not the economy. Not health care. Not climate change. Not education. Nothing.

But here is an interesting fact. Despite Trump's hateful and inflammatory rhetoric, it turns out that undocumented immigrants have a lower crime rate in this country than people who are born here. The Brennan Center reports: "Substantial research has assessed the relationship between immigration and crime. Numerous studies show that immigration is not linked to higher levels of crime, but rather the opposite. Studies have also examined the impact of the concentration of immigrants in a community on crime patterns, finding that immigration is associated with lower crime rates and an increase in structural factors—such as social connection and economic opportunity—that are linked to neighborhood safety."

Alex Nowrasteh, an immigration policy analyst at the Cato Institute, a conservative think tank in Washington, D.C., told *USA Today*: "The findings show pretty consistently undocumented and illegal immigrants have a lower conviction rate and are less likely to be convicted of homicide and other crimes overall compared to native-born Americans in Texas."

And here's something else that's interesting. Despite his supposed concern about crime and law and order, Trump failed to mention the assailant who attempted the most significant criminal act of the year, the assassination of a presidential candidate. Why that omission? Well, maybe it has something to do with the fact that the young man who shot at Trump was a white American born in the U.S.A.

The reality is that the overwhelming majority of undocumented people in this country not only obey the law but also play an extremely important part in maintaining our economy. During COVID, many of the undocumented were the "essential workers" that kept our economy from collapsing. More than a few died as a result of those jobs.

The Catholic Church, here in the United States and internationally, has been strong and consistent in defending the immigrant community. In a speech in Chicago in June 2025, Cardinal Blase Cupich stated: "It is wrong to scapegoat those who are here without documents. For indeed, they are here due to a broken immigration system. And it is a broken immigration system which both parties have failed to fix." He continued: "So many of the undocumented have for decades been connected to us. They are here not by invasion, but by invitation—an invitation to harvest the fruits of the earth that feed our families; an invitation to clean our tables, homes and hotel rooms; an invitation to landscape our lawns; and yes, even an invitation to care for our children and elders."

I couldn't agree more. It is absolutely imperative that we vigorously expose Trump's demagogic efforts to demonize the undocumented. That is why I am doing everything I can not only to oppose

Trump's ugly immigration policies, but to move toward comprehensive immigration reform that protects those who are in the country now and provides them with an eventual path toward citizenship. Trump wants us to hate each other. I want us to come together to take on Trump and his oligarch friends.

Much of the discussion about Trump's "Big Beautiful Bill" dealt with tax breaks for billionaires and massive cuts to Medicaid, nutrition, and education. All enormously important. But what often got neglected in analyzing that legislation was another provision, of perhaps even greater consequence. The bill contains a massive $75 billion in funding for Immigration and Customs Enforcement (ICE) that will make it, by far, the largest federal law enforcement agency in America—bigger than the FBI and the DEA combined. This paves the way, for the first time in our history, for the creation of a huge, well-armed domestic military force.

This is an extremely dangerous precedent. It means that, under an authoritarian president who lies all of the time, we will have many thousands of federal agents patrolling our streets and combing our neighborhoods. It is bad enough that we have a president who is usurping the powers of Congress, who has ended dissent within the Republican Party, who is intimidating the courts, law firms, the media, and universities. We now have, ostensibly in search of undocumented immigrants, a domestic army of thousands of well-armed agents obeying his every command.

Trump's Big Lies serve a larger purpose. They are part of the growth of oligarchy and authoritarianism that is not limited just to the United States. Sadly, this reality is taking hold throughout the world.

3

GLOBAL OLIGARCHY: BILLIONAIRES WIN, THE WORLD SUFFERS

The rapid movement to oligarchy, income and wealth inequality, and authoritarianism is not just taking place in America. It is a global phenomenon and the most important economic and political reality of our time. Today, a tiny handful of the richest people on Earth have extraordinary power over the lives of billions of inhabitants in virtually every country on Earth. And, increasingly, it is not elected governments that regulate the activities of billionaires. It is the unelected billionaire class that influences the activities and policies of government.

The result: Oligarchy is ascending, inequality is growing, and democracy is in decline.

And let's be clear. In an increasingly globalized economy, the allegiance of these oligarchs is not to their own nations. It is to their own power. It is to their own bank accounts. It is to their huge yachts, their mansions, their fancy cars, their private islands, and their fleet of jets.

Document leaks like the Paradise Papers, the Panama Papers, and the Pandora Papers have uncovered a staggering scale of money laundering, kleptocracy, and tax avoidance by the richest people in the world. UC Berkeley economist Gabriel Zucman estimates that at the end of 2022, at least $12 trillion in private household wealth was hidden in offshore tax havens throughout the world. Twelve trillion dollars! As economist Brooke Harrington notes, that represents roughly 12 percent of all the wealth produced in the world that year.

While governments throughout the world struggle to produce budgets that can serve the needs of their people, the billionaires hide their money in tax havens, refuse to pay their fair share of taxes—and children go hungry. For the oligarchs, the only people that matter are themselves. They are extremely religious people. But unlike in other religions, their god is money. And greed is their value system. They are not nice people.

If the workers of the world have not yet united, as Marx had hoped they would, the oligarchs surely have. In a world of more than 8 billion people, a network of a few thousand multibillionaires are dividing up the globe amongst themselves. Never before in modern history have so few had so much wealth and so much power, while so many live in desperation.

The United States, with 902 billionaires, is the center of global oligarchy. It is the home to more billionaires than any other country. The seven wealthiest people in the world, and fourteen out of the fifteen richest people on the planet, with a combined net worth of more than $2.6 trillion, call America their home. And since Trump was elected president, the four wealthiest people on the planet

(Elon Musk, Larry Ellison, Mark Zuckerberg, and Jeff Bezos) have become more than $200 billion richer. Further, they have been given the keys to the federal government and the media world after contributing hundreds of millions of dollars to the Republican Party and Trump himself.

Income and wealth inequality, however, are not just an American issue. Today, according to researchers at Oxfam and other organizations, we live in a world where the top 1 percent own more wealth than the bottom 95 percent of humanity. In truth, that is likely a conservative estimate, as much of the wealth of these oligarchs is stashed in secret tax-haven accounts. Meanwhile, as the very rich become richer, the gap between them and the world's impoverished is growing wider.

Over the past five years, 5 billion people throughout the world have become poorer, while the five richest people on the planet have more than tripled their wealth and are now worth a combined $1.34 trillion. That's trillion with a *T*.

While nearly half of the world's population—over 3.7 billion people—live in poverty, trying to survive on less than seven dollars a day, just 3,000 billionaires throughout the globe have seen their wealth explode by more than $6.5 trillion since 2015. Incredibly, those 3,000 people who comprise the global billionaire class own more wealth than the GDP of every country in the world—except the United States and China. In other words, the combined wealth of these 3,000 people would make them the third wealthiest country on Earth.

All over the world, hundreds of millions of desperate people are unable to access food, clean drinking water, adequate health care, decent housing, or education. Children by the millions die of easily preventable diseases. Meanwhile, the world's top 1 percent have become $33.9 trillion richer since 2015. That, by the way, is enough money to eliminate world poverty twenty-two times over.

Let's take a quick look at how oligarchy exists throughout the world.

Russia: Yachts, Palaces, and a Population in Poverty

If there is one area of the world where the Establishment is comfortable using the term "oligarchy," it is Russia. And, in this case, they are absolutely correct. In many respects, Russia has become the model for what an oligarchic authoritarian society looks like. Vladimir Putin is not only an autocrat who kills his political opponents to stay in power, he is also one of the wealthiest people in the world.

In 2017, Putin, at the head of a kleptocratic government, was estimated to be worth $200 billion. He owns a $700 million, 270-foot-long super yacht that is equipped with a gym, a saloon, a spa, a library, two helipads, and a 49-foot indoor pool that can be converted into a dance floor. He also owns a $1.4 billion palace on the Black Sea with a casino, private theater, and underground hockey rink.

And, among the oligarchs in Russia, Putin is not alone. After the fall of the Soviet Union, the

Boris Yeltsin regime initiated the largest privatization scheme in world history. State-owned industries were sold off to Yeltsin's allies for pennies on the dollar—and they made a fortune as a result.

Today, while over 13 million Russians live in poverty, the wealthiest 500 Russians possess more wealth than the bottom 99.8 percent of the population—145 million people. Not only do these great Russian "patriots" stash an enormous amount of their wealth in hidden offshore tax havens and foreign real estate, but they seem to have an obsession with giant yachts. While more than a dozen yachts owned by Russian oligarchs have been seized through international sanctions as a result of the war in Ukraine, many have not. Some thirty-two yachts owned by Russian oligarchs have found safe harbor in Turkey, the Seychelles, Montenegro, and the Maldives.

Russia is a prime example of how oligarchy, authoritarianism, and kleptocracy merge. It's not a pretty sight. But Russia is not unique.

The Middle East: Royalty and the Rise of the Super-Rich

In the Middle East, the story is equally disturbing. As a result of vast oil and gas reserves, this region contains five of the world's ten richest monarchs. One of them is the emir of Qatar, Sheikh Tamim bin Hamad Al Thani. In May 2025, Donald Trump accepted a $400 million airplane from the royal family of Qatar—just one more example of Trump's kleptocratic practices. But this $400 million gift was a small investment for a family worth an estimated $335 billion. Led by Sheikh Tamim, the family owns a fleet of fourteen aircraft and resides in a $1 billion royal estate with fifteen palaces and a collection of over five hundred cars—including Lamborghinis, Ferraris, Rolls-Royces, and Mercedes. In London, they own a $140 million super-mansion with seventeen bedrooms, fourteen lounges, a cinema, a juice bar, and a swimming pool. They also possess one of the world's most expensive yachts—valued at $400 million.

While the royal family of Qatar lives in unimaginable opulence, how do they treat the people who work for them and helped create their wealth? Well, a ten-year investigation by *The Guardian* found that at least 6,500 workers from some of the poorest parts of the world, including Nepal and North Korea, died under extremely unsafe working conditions as they built a state-of-the-art soccer stadium, luxury hotels, buildings, and roads after Qatar was awarded the right to host the World Cup in 2022. Many other migrant workers were paid pennies an hour, forced into debt, and had their passports confiscated until they completed their jobs.

Meanwhile, in Saudi Arabia, the House of Saud is considered to be the wealthiest family in the world, with an estimated $1.4 trillion fortune coming primarily from the country's vast oil reserves and Saudi Aramco, the state-owned oil company. While Mohammed bin Salman, the crown prince of Saudi Arabia, has been able to afford a $500 million yacht, a $450 million painting by Leonardo da

Vinci, and a $500 billion luxury city in the desert, the youth unemployment in his country exceeds 30 percent. More ominously, Saudi Arabia is considered one of the worst human rights violators in the world as it detains, tortures, and executes women's rights activists and others who peacefully advocate for change. Not too many demonstrators outside the royal palace.

And, like Qatar, the wealth of the kingdom is dependent upon the horrific exploitation of impoverished foreign labor. Since construction began on Neom, Saudi Arabia's megacity of the future, an estimated 21,000 migrant workers have died. The majority of the deceased are from impoverished countries like Nepal, India, and Bangladesh. Over 14,000 Indian workers alone have lost their lives. In addition to fatalities, migrant workers face horrific conditions on the job, including wage theft and grueling hours in the hot sun.

Southeast Asia: A One-Man Show

And then there is Brunei, in Southeast Asia, a country of fewer than half a million people led by Hassanal Bolkiah, the sultan of Brunei. While millions of people throughout the region live in poverty, the sultan is worth at least $30 billion. In Russia, the oligarchs are obsessed with yachts. Not the sultan. His big thing is cars—lots of them. He owns 7,000 cars, including 600 Rolls-Royces, 450 Ferraris, and 380 Bentleys. He also has a rather nice home, a palace worth $350 million with 1,788 rooms, 257 bathrooms, five swimming pools, 51,000 light bulbs, and 564 chandeliers. And when the sultan is able to find his way out of his palace, he is a very busy guy. He is the country's prime minister, finance minister, defense minister, and minister of foreign affairs. Oligarchy, kleptocracy, and authoritarianism are alive and well in Brunei.

The United Kingdom: The British Billionaire Empire

Across the ocean in the United Kingdom, 156 billionaires now hold more than $835 billion. The richest fifty people in Great Britain control more wealth than the bottom half of the entire country—over 34 million people.

Further, foreign oligarchs are buying up major parts of London and other British cities, making housing unaffordable for working families. As a result of major cuts in domestic spending for the needs of working families, the child poverty rate in Britain has skyrocketed. Today, an estimated 31 percent of British children (4.5 million in total) live in poverty, the highest number since at least 2002.

Africa: A Continent of Rich Resources and Desperately Poor People

For centuries, the slave trade and colonization wreaked havoc and horror on this vast continent.

Today, Africa is perhaps the most tragic example of the pain that oligarchy can inflict.

In 2000, Africa had zero billionaires. Today it has twenty-three, and their combined wealth has increased by over 50 percent in just the past five years. Incredibly, the four wealthiest men in Africa now control $57.4 billion, which is more wealth than that of the bottom 750 million people there—half of the population.

And while the wealth of Africa's billionaires grows, so has hunger. In 2023, nearly 850 million people in Africa experienced food insecurity. That's an increase of 20 million in just one year. While Africa is rich in natural resources—from diamonds to oil—seven out of every ten people living in extreme poverty today can be found in Africa.

Meanwhile, African governments collect just 0.3 percent of GDP in taxes from the wealthy—the lowest rate in the world—while imposing regressive taxes on its citizens that punish the poor and reward the rich.

Mexico: One Guy Owns Almost All of It

In Mexico, Carlos Slim, the richest man in the country, is worth more than $96 billion. Yes. In a nation where millions of impoverished Mexicans have migrated to the United States in search of a better life, one man owns more wealth than the bottom half of the country—65 million people.

Slim built his empire through monopoly control of telecommunications as a result of privatization and his connections to the government. He successfully lobbied to keep his competitors out and prices incredibly high—in a country where millions still lack access to the internet or phones, and over 35 percent of its people live in poverty.

India: Billionaires Dominate, the Poor Suffer

India now has the largest population in the world, with 1.46 billion people. It also has over 200 billionaires, whose combined wealth surged to $941 billion in 2025. Meanwhile, over 75 million people in India live in extreme poverty—trying to survive on just three dollars a day.

One of the wealthiest men in India is Gautam Adani, a coal and infrastructure oligarch and close ally of Prime Minister Narendra Modi, a right-wing autocrat. Adani used his connections with Modi to win billions of dollars in contracts, huge tax breaks, the deregulation of his coal operation, the suppression of labor unions, and a friendly court system that has delayed investigations into his companies.

Meanwhile, tens of millions of people in India lack access to health care, education, nutritious food, and decent-paying jobs.

Our Planet Cannot Continue to Be Owned by the Oligarchs

In country after country, continent after continent, we now see unprecedented levels of income and wealth inequality, and more and more political power in the hands of the oligarchs. Despite all the revolutions, elections, and international conferences of the last 150 years, planet Earth and its 8 billion inhabitants are now largely controlled by a few thousand ultra-rich individuals.

While working families throughout the world struggle to put food on the table, and billions live in extreme, life-threatening poverty, the oligarchs build palaces and show off their yachts, fancy cars, and expensive art collections. They vacation on their own islands and, when they get bored, take joyrides into outer space. Through the rigged economic system they created, they have more money than they could spend in a thousand lifetimes. How pathetic!

As the late Pope Francis noted in a speech at the Vatican in 2013: "We have created new idols. The worship of the golden calf of old has found a new and heartless image in the cult of money and the dictatorship of an economy which is faceless and lacking any truly humane goal." He continued: "Today everything comes under the laws of competition and the survival of the fittest, where the powerful feed upon the powerless. As a consequence, masses of people find themselves excluded and marginalized: without work, without possibilities, without any means of escape."

Pope Francis was right. We are "lacking any truly humane goal." And if humanity is going to survive, that must change. We cannot continue having a handful of multibillionaires running the world for their own selfish interests.

4

THEY DID IT THEN, WE CAN DO IT NOW

SOME LESSONS FROM HISTORY

Nelson Mandela said it best: "It always seems impossible until it is done." In other words, in the midst of a struggle the prospect of victory often seems far removed. But after victory, no one seems surprised.

There is no doubt that we are living in a very dangerous, frightening, and tumultuous moment in modern American history.

If you're feeling overwhelmed or stressed-out about the direction that Donald Trump and his band of oligarchs and right-wing authoritarians are taking this country, you're not alone. Millions of Americans feel the same way.

But as difficult as things may seem now, it is extremely important to remind ourselves that this is by no means the first daunting crisis that our country has faced. And it is even more important to remember that with courage, intelligence, hard work, and discipline, those previous crises and injustices were overcome.

The main political goal of the Establishment is to make you feel that you're powerless. That resistance is hopeless. That there is nothing you can do to change the difficult situations that we face. If they succeed in making you feel that way, they will win now—and always. Don't let them accomplish that goal. Fight back.

I am not a historian, but I think it's important that, in this unprecedented moment in modern American history, we learn from the past and remember that much of the history of the United States is a history of struggle—of ordinary people coming together to challenge entrenched power, to confront injustice, and to accomplish what the political and economic establishments of the time insisted could not be done.

When we stand together, we win. When the ruling class divides us up, we lose. That is one of the great lessons of history that we must never forget.

A few examples serve as a reminder of what is possible.

Taking on the King of England

I am not a romantic, and I do not believe that this country is "exceptional" and provided with God-given blessings. But I do know that, as Americans, we have a right to be extremely proud of how and why this nation was created in the 1770s, the men and women who made it happen, and how their efforts made this new nation an inspiration for people throughout the globe.

In the 1770s, American colonists stood up to the most powerful monarchy in the world, which saw them as little more than subjects to be taxed and exploited. In the beginning of that struggle they had no regular army, no navy, and very little wealth compared to the British Empire. Further, a significant minority of people in the colonies supported the Crown and opposed the movement for independence. The American revolutionaries had no international support. They were on their own.

But if they lacked a military as strong as the British, they had something their adversary could not compete with. They had a vision that rejected the "divine right of kings" and a passionate belief that "all men are created equal" and are entitled to "Life, Liberty and the pursuit of Happiness." They were prepared to fight and die for these principles; as they wrote in the Declaration of Independence, "Whenever any Form of Government becomes destructive of these ends, it is the Right of the People to alter or to abolish it." Wow! That was in 1776. Pretty powerful stuff!

With extraordinary courage, our forefathers declared independence and inspired thirteen colonies to fight the American Revolution. And the rest is history. The independence movement of thirteen struggling colonies was able to defeat the most powerful ruler in the world.

They did it then. We can and will do it now.

The Abolitionist Movement and the Fight for Racial Justice

But as we all know, the Declaration of Independence, the Revolutionary War, and the Constitution were not the end of the fight to move this country forward in the never-ending pursuit of liberty, justice, and freedom. It was just the beginning.

Decades later, that fire for justice continued to burn in the hearts of abolitionists like Frederick Douglass, Harriet Tubman, William Lloyd Garrison, Sojourner Truth, and John Quincy Adams.

These courageous men and women rose up not only against the horrors and brutality of slavery, but also against the obvious contradiction inherent in a nation claiming to be "the land of the free." How could America be "free," they demanded to know, when millions of inhabitants were treated as chattel, bought and sold with absolutely no human rights?

In the North, the abolitionists were often attacked as radicals, and were given little chance of success. In the South, the abolitionists were opposed by the entire ruling class, whose wealth and power rested upon the foundation of slavery.

It took a brutal civil war and many hundreds of thousands of deaths, but the abolitionists prevailed. Slavery was abolished.

Yet that victory was not the end of the story. Not by a long shot. Out of slavery came the horrors of Jim Crow—a new regime of segregation and racial apartheid that denied Black Americans their most basic rights. Black Americans could not vote or go to the same schools, restaurants, hotels, or bathrooms as whites. The jobs they were allowed to have paid substantially lower wages than similar work done by whites. They were told by the Establishment that "separate but equal" was the best we could achieve as a nation. Anything else was impossible.

When Dr. Martin Luther King Jr., John Lewis, A. Philip Randolph, and countless others stood up to this injustice, they were called "communists." They were investigated by the FBI. They were met with violence, arrests, and institutional resistance. Some of them were killed.

In 1963, the governor of Alabama, George Wallace, declared: "Segregation now, segregation tomorrow, segregation forever." It didn't quite happen the way Wallace wanted.

Thanks to the civil rights movement in which millions of Americans, Black and white, demonstrated, marched, sat in, and filled up jails, one year after Wallace's racist declaration President Lyndon Johnson signed the Civil Rights Act of 1964. That legislation outlawed discrimination based on race, color, religion, sex, or national origin. A year later, he signed the Voting Rights Act of 1965 to prohibit racial discrimination in voting.

They did it then. We can and will do it now.

The Fight for Workers' Rights

Most workers understand that if you want decent wages, working conditions, and benefits, you can't get them by yourself. You have to join with your coworkers, form a union, and bargain collectively for a decent contract. That is true today, in a time when unions are more popular than they have been for decades. That was true 150 years ago.

Workers have always understood the power of unions. So have their bosses. And that's why the growth of the trade union movement in America is a history of struggle, sacrifice, and extraordinary courage in the face of corporate greed and power.

Let us not forget that in the nineteenth century, as America industrialized, millions of workers and their children toiled in brutal conditions, sometimes working ten or twelve hours a day, six or seven days a week, for starvation wages. No health care, no safety standards, no job security, no rights.

And the workers fought back.

In 1886, Chicago workers organized to demand

an eight-hour workday, an idea that at that time was considered extremely radical. Their request was simple: "Eight hours for work, eight hours for rest, eight hours for what we will." At a labor rally in Haymarket Square in support of the eight-hour workday, a bomb exploded. Several workers and police officers were killed in the melee that followed. A number of labor leaders were arrested, even though there was no evidence tying them to the violence. Four of them were eventually executed. Why were they executed? Because the bosses wanted to make an example of them, and make it clear that there would be dire consequences for any worker who stood up and fought for his or her rights.

Those four labor leaders were unjustly executed for a crime they didn't commit. They lost their lives, but as a result of that struggle, the eight-hour workday was eventually established and became the law of the land.

Just two years before, the Pullman Company (which manufactured luxury railroad sleeping cars) slashed wages and refused to lower outrageously high rents in company-owned housing. In response, workers walked off their jobs. The American Railway Union, led by Eugene V. Debs—one of the great leaders of the working class in American history—called for a nationwide boycott of trains pulling Pullman cars. The federal government, at the behest of the railroad bosses, sent in troops. Violence erupted, and dozens of workers were killed. Debs went to prison and the workers lost the strike.

But that struggle, which brought about a national boycott against Pullman cars involving some 250,000 workers, showed the country the power of labor solidarity and the growing strength of organized labor. It also resulted in the creation of Labor Day as a federal holiday.

In 1914, in Ludlow, Colorado, members of the United Mine Workers of America (UMWA) went out on strike demanding better pay and protections against the extremely dangerous working conditions in the mines. The coal company responded by evicting them from their company-owned homes. On April 20, National Guardsmen aligned with the company attempted to break the strike by attacking the tents where workers and their children were forced to live. They killed twenty-one people (including eleven children) in what became known as the Ludlow Massacre. This act, so deadly for the union members and their children, focused national attention on the terrible conditions that many workers were facing, and was instrumental in ending child labor in the country.

And here's a simple truth: When unions are strong, working families do better. From 1946 to the late 1970s, the standard of living of the American working class rose significantly. That was no accident. That was the direct result of a successful trade union movement bargaining for better wages, benefits, and working conditions. And let's be clear. Collective bargaining wasn't just good for union members. It helped lift wages and benefits for the entire working class. In fact, thanks to the trade union movement, during that period a vibrant middle class in this country was created that for years was the envy of the world.

Over the last two hundred years, trade unionists have been beaten by police, company thugs, and National Guardsmen. Their families have been pushed into extreme deprivation by prolonged strikes. They have been jailed and even killed in the fight for economic justice. But as a result of their determination, they gave this country an eight-hour workday, the end of child labor, safer working conditions, a minimum wage, and strong retirement and health care benefits for millions of their members. And while there is still a ton of unfinished business left to be done, we owe a debt of gratitude to the trade union movement for the extraordinary victories it achieved.

They did it then. We can and will do it now.

The Struggle for Women's Rights

Let's not forget. When the Constitution of the United States was written, women in America were not just treated as second-class citizens; they were treated as third-class citizens. They were denied the right to vote; the right to employment opportunities; the right to an education; and, in many states, the right to own property. Domestic violence was considered a "family matter."

When suffragists like Susan B. Anthony, Lucretia Mott, Elizabeth Cady Stanton, and Sojourner Truth demanded that women receive the right to vote, they were ridiculed. They were told that "politics is no place for a woman." They were told that men were able to run the government and "take care of the women."

And yet, despite the widespread sexism at that time, they fought on. They lobbied intensely, they petitioned, they marched, they engaged in civil disobedience, they went on hunger strikes, and they went to jail. And as a result of their persistence and courage, they won. In 1920, the Nineteenth Amendment granted women the right to vote. And since then, while much more needs to be done, barrier after barrier—to employment opportunities, education, financial opportunities, and political participation—has been broken down.

They did it then. We can and will do it now.

The Fight for Free Public Education

In the early 1800s, schools were reserved for the children of the wealthy. If you were poor, if you were a farmer's kid or a factory worker's child, you were expected to work—period. A formal education was not for you. There were only private schools for the children of the rich.

But the working class of America fought back and demanded free public education for all. In the late 1820s, labor leaders like William Heighton, George Henry Evans, Noah Cook, and Henry Guyon helped establish the Working Men's Party with major branches in Philadelphia, New York, and Boston. They ran on a working-class platform that called for, among other pro-worker proposals, the creation of free public schools for children, open to all regardless of income. And while the working-class party they established was short-lived, through relentless organizing and advocacy, their goal was achieved.

In 1827, Massachusetts became the first state in the nation to establish a system of free public education. In 1834, the state legislature in Pennsylvania passed the Free School Act, which offered primary education to every child without the need to declare their financial status. By 1847, not only were public schools in New York City free for children, regardless of income, but the Free Academy was created (which later became the City College of New York) to provide a free higher education to all. City by city, state by state, free public education systems were established. By the early twentieth century, free K–12 education became the norm in most of the country.

They did it then. We can and will do it now.

The Fight for LGBT Rights

It wasn't that long ago that being gay in America was a crime. People were jailed, suffered physical violence, and lost their jobs. As a result, millions of Americans were forced to hide their sexual orientation and their personal relationships.

After centuries of persecution, the LGBT community stood up and fought back. A notable event in that struggle took place on June 28, 1969, when gay patrons at the Stonewall Inn in New York City, after years of harassment, physically resisted a police raid. Days of open protest against LGBT discrimination followed. The Stonewall rebellion paved the way for gay pride parades across the country, the growth of gay organizations, and more and more gay people "coming out of the closet."

It also helped lead to legislation legalizing gay marriage. Vermont was the first state to establish civil unions for same-sex couples, in 2000. In 2004, as the result of a court decision, Massachusetts became the first state to legalize gay marriage, followed by thirty-six other states. In 2015, same-sex marriage was legalized nationwide through the Supreme Court's decision in *Obergefell v. Hodges*.

Fifty years ago, very few people would have imagined that gay marriage would ever become the law of the land. But it happened. It happened because people in the LGBT community, and their straight allies, showed enormous courage—and succeeded in convincing the American people that discrimination based on sexual orientation was wrong, and not what America was supposed to be about.

They did it then. We can and will do it now.

Lessons from the Past, Hope for the Future

The reality is that, throughout history, each and every time ordinary people stood up and fought injustice, the wealthy and the powerful told them to sit down and shut up. They were told that real change was impossible. They were fired from their jobs, assailed by the media, jailed, assaulted, and sometimes even killed.

But they fought on—and they won.

Frederick Douglass said it best: "Power concedes nothing without a demand. It never did and it never will. Find out just what any people will quietly submit to and you have found out the exact measure of injustice and wrong which will be imposed upon them, and these will continue till they are resisted with either words or blows, or with both. The limits of tyrants are prescribed by the endurance of those whom they oppress."

Those words are as true today as they were back when Douglass first said them in 1857.

5

FIGHTING OLIGARCHY

The size and energy of the crowds was something that I had never seen before. As a candidate for president, I have done many campaign swings, and held rallies in almost every state in the country. Some of them were very large. But nothing like this.

We started planning the Fighting Oligarchy tour in late January of 2025—not long after Trump was inaugurated. Our goal: Make it clear that large numbers of Americans, in blue states and red states, were prepared to stand up and fight back against oligarchy, authoritarianism, kleptocracy, and the war against the working class of our country.

The most powerful tool the ruling class has to protect their interests is to make ordinary people feel powerless. Their message: *You are alone and there is nothing you, or anyone else, can do to stop us. We have the wealth. We have the power. We will prevail. Just shut up and get out of the way.*

That was the enormously powerful narrative that we were determined to overcome.

Our first stop was in Omaha, Nebraska, on February 21. How many people would show up in a district with a Republican congressman, a Republican governor, a Republican statehouse, and two Republican senators? We had no idea. We located a local union hall to host the event that accommodated about 800 people. The RSVPs started coming in and we soon realized it wouldn't work. We moved to a hotel ballroom that accommodated 2,600, but on the night of the event, we still had to turn away some 800 people—in Omaha, Nebraska. We were off and running.

The next day, we were in Iowa City, another Republican district. The crowd was so large that we had to do two separate events a block away from each other. The overflow crowd was actually larger than the original venue could hold.

Two weeks later, we did events in Kenosha and Altoona, Wisconsin. Once again, great turnouts. What was special about those events, however, was not only that we were talking about oligarchy, but that we were actually taking it on. Elon Musk was in the process of spending millions in the state to fund a right-wing, anti-choice candidate in a Wisconsin Supreme Court election. Musk's involvement in a state election made clear to everyone in Wisconsin, as well as more and more people around the country, what oligarchy was all about. The richest person in the world was trying to buy an election. I was happy to support the candidate that Musk opposed, Susan Crawford, who eventually went on to win.

The turnouts in Kenosha and Altoona were very strong. But the attendance in Warren, Michigan, on the evening of March 8, was amazing. I was joined at the rally by Shawn Fain, president of the United Auto Workers (UAW), and Dr. Abdul El-Sayed, a former progressive candidate for governor of Michigan.

Four months earlier, at the height of the general election, Trump had come to Warren and brought out some 4,000 people. Now we had brought out 9,000. Without any of us being a candidate for anything, we were doubling the turnout that Trump drew in his campaign. Yes. No question about it. People were fired up about fighting oligarchy.

What was also interesting was that our events were not just attracting progressives and my supporters. My campaign has lists of millions of names, and we pretty much know which of our supporters come to our events. It turned out that about 60 percent of the attendees were not on our lists. And 30 percent were either Independents or Republicans. People of all political persuasions were outraged at what's going on in Washington.

The turnout and excitement generated by the

events in Nebraska, Iowa, Wisconsin, and Michigan had us thinking big. We started planning for a series of events in the Southwest. And, on this trip, we took a special guest along with us.

Alexandria Ocasio-Cortez is an outstanding progressive member of Congress from New York City. In 2018, despite being an absolute political novice and having no money, she ran a brilliant grassroots campaign and defeated one of the most powerful politicians in the state and a leader of the Democratic Party in Congress. Upon taking office, she revolutionized, through social media, how a member of Congress communicates with constituents. Her boldness, intelligence, and charisma, not to mention her standing up for the working class of this country, has galvanized an entire generation of young people and helped bring millions into the political process.

I asked Alexandria to join us for the next Fighting Oligarchy swing, and she was excited to do it.

What I should point out here is that our choice of rally locations was, with some exceptions, targeted at Republican districts. In doing that, we had several goals. First, we wanted to put pressure on Republican members of Congress who had won their last election by a small margin. Our immediate hope was to convince them to vote against the disastrous Republican reconciliation bill that proposed massive cuts to health care, nutrition, and education while giving huge tax breaks to the very rich. Further, we wanted to lay the groundwork in those districts for a movement of people who could mobilize for the 2026 election and defeat Republican incumbents. As of this writing, Republicans hold a very slim majority in the U.S. House. If we can defeat five of them, they will lose control over Congress, and we can take a major step forward in stopping Trump's dangerous agenda.

Perhaps most importantly, the goal of these rallies is to make people understand that they are not alone. Standing alongside thousands of other people in your community who share your belief that a handful of billionaires should not be running your country gives people strength and hope. They learn what the Establishment does not want them to know. That their views are not fringe. That in fact they are part of the majority. Yes, in the United States we can and must have a government and an economy that works for all, not just the few. Yes, in the richest nation on Earth, health care and education should be a human right available to everyone. Yes, we must combat the existential threat of climate change. No, 800,000 Americans should not be homeless.

On March 20, 2025, Alexandria and I began our Southwest tour. And what a trip it was. Over 3,000 people came to an outdoor rally in Las Vegas, the largest turnout we have ever had in Nevada. Later that evening we traveled to Tempe, Arizona, where 15,000 people filled a basketball arena to capacity. The next day, we did a beautiful outdoor event in Greeley, Colorado, at the University of Northern Colorado, where 11,000 people showed up. And then we raced to Denver for an evening event. And, let me tell you, that was absolutely insane.

During my two presidential campaigns, we put together some very large rallies. In New York City we had brought out 25,000 people, and in Los Angeles a bit more. Huge crowds. But nothing compared to Denver. It was a turnout of 34,000. Standing at the podium, I literally could not see the end of that crowd. It was massive. It was loud. It was joyful. It was full of people prepared to fight for fundamental change in our country.

The next day, March 22, we completed the Southwest tour with a rally in Tucson, Arizona—another extraordinary event. We rented out a football stadium at Catalina High School. We thought that would be big enough. It wasn't. People kept coming and coming. The bleachers were filled, and people flowed onto the playing field. Over 23,000 showed up—in Tucson, Arizona.

Needless to say, these rallies drew an enormous amount of local and national media attention. They were also making the Republicans nervous. Not surprisingly, they responded with lies. Musk posted that many of the 34,000 who came to our

Denver rally were "paid organizers." Trump was busy boasting, falsely, that his turnouts were always larger than ours.

Three weeks later, Alexandria and I began our West Coast tour. Those events were the most successful, exciting, and impactful that I've ever done in my life.

In Los Angeles, we had speakers from all of the major unions in the state. We had great music as well: a wonderful gospel choir, as well as Maggie Rogers and legendary singers Neil Young and Joan Baez. Congressmembers Jimmy Gomez, Maxwell Frost, Pramila Jayapal, and Ro Khanna also joined Alexandria and me. It was quite the event. Thirty-six thousand people showed up—the largest rally turnout that I've ever been part of.

After Los Angeles, we hit the road and drove three hours to Indio, California, where the singer Clairo invited me to introduce her onstage at the Coachella music festival. In my five-minute introductory remarks, I urged young people to get involved in the political process, and reminded them to join Clairo in speaking out against immoral wars like the horrific humanitarian disaster in Gaza. From the crowd, I heard several shout, "Fight the Oligarchy!" The message was spreading.

After Coachella, Alexandria and I headed to two very conservative states—places where the Democratic Party virtually does not exist. In Salt Lake City, Utah, we brought out 20,000 people. Yes. Twenty thousand people in Utah. The next night, we went to perhaps the reddest state in the country: Idaho. And, believe it or not, 12,500 people came out for our rally in Nampa.

The next day, April 15, 2025, was perhaps the most amazing day of the campaign. To be honest, the only thing that I knew about Folsom, California, was that Johnny Cash had recorded a live album at the prison there. I also knew that Folsom had a Republican member of Congress. Frankly, in a million years, I never would've guessed that 30,000 people would turn out in this rural community—but that's exactly what happened.

Our West Coast trip ended with a very

well-attended event in Missoula, Montana—another Republican state.

I spent May Day in Philadelphia, and held rallies in Harrisburg and Bethlehem with congressman Chris Deluzio. And by the time June rolled around, we were preparing to head out to Texas.

Texas is, in my view, the most important state in the country from a political perspective. In many respects, as Texas goes, so goes America. And Texas *should* be going progressive. More than 40 percent of the state is Latino. Combined with a large Black population, well over half of the state are people of color—almost all of whom are working-class. With its growing population of young people and the strength of its trade union movement, the state should be a progressive stronghold, not right-wing. But for many years the Democratic Party in the state has done a terrible job. There is new leadership there now, and I hope things will change.

Our first stop in Texas was in McAllen, near the border, with Texas congressman Greg Casar—a strong progressive and the head of the

Congressional Progressive Caucus. I learned a lot in McAllen, a city with a large Latino population. I learned that since Trump started his raids on immigrant communities across the country, people in McAllen—hardworking people who had lived there for years—were so terrified of being swept into an unmarked van by a group of masked men that they simply did not go out after dark. The downtown was largely deserted.

For these people, Trump's policies were not an abstraction. They were living the ugly reality of those policies, and I could feel the heavy weight and burden that the community carried. It will stay with me for a long time.

From there we went to Louisiana and the backyard of Speaker Mike Johnson—the architect of the most destructive piece of legislation in modern history, Trump's "Big Beautiful Bill." I wanted the people there to fully understand what their representative in Congress was doing, and how it impacted their lives. In Shreveport, the crowd was fired up. Nearly 2,000 people—in one of the reddest districts in America—came out to voice their disgust with our rigged economy and the legislation that would give the top 1 percent a trillion dollars in tax breaks and almost certainly shut down rural hospitals and nursing homes in their communities.

Next we headed to Tulsa, Oklahoma. As I prepared to finish my speech to a fired-up crowd of 5,500 people, my campaign manager rushed onstage with a printout of a statement from Trump that began: "We have completed our very successful attack on the three Nuclear sites in Iran."

I read the statement to the audience and a deafening chorus of boos rang out. And, in unison, the crowd began to chant: "No More War. No More War." It was an incredibly powerful moment that was caught in a video that went viral. Over 15 million people viewed it. The people in Tulsa, and people throughout America, were tired of endless wars.

After the rally, I got on the phone with my staff to organize a response to Trump's attack and put together legislation to prohibit the use of federal funds for any military force in or against Iran without specific congressional authorization. While I worked with my staff to prevent the United States from being dragged into another war, I had to miss our rally in Amarillo, Texas. Fortunately, both Greg Casar and former congressman Beto O'Rourke were there.

Our last stop in Texas was in Fort Worth, where I was joined by Greg and Beto. It was a great event with more than 6,000 Texans showing up in a Republican-held district.

By the end of July, almost 280,000 people had attended twenty-four Fighting Oligarchy rallies in Nebraska, Iowa, Michigan, Wisconsin, Colorado, Nevada, California, Utah, Idaho, Montana, Arizona, Pennsylvania, Texas, Louisiana, and Oklahoma.

But it's important to know that our goal in doing these rallies was not just to parachute in, bring out a lot of people, and leave. It was to help build a movement.

Every time we left a state, we followed up with

the attendees and gave them opportunities to get involved in the political process. Sometimes it was demanding that a member of Congress hold a town hall meeting to answer their questions. Sometimes it was asking people to go door-to-door, distributing literature and educating their neighbors about what was going on in Washington. In states like Colorado, Utah, and California, we asked people to get involved in fights important to organized labor. In other words, these rallies were the beginning of our efforts—not the end.

We hired full-time organizers in Nebraska, Iowa, Wisconsin, and Michigan to put together town halls, canvasses, protests, and call-in campaigns targeting their Republican members of Congress.

Through our email lists and online training, we mobilized thousands of volunteers to do the same in Republican states and districts across the country.

We were also working hard to get progressives to run for office—from school board, to city council, to state legislature, to the U.S. Congress. We reached out to everyone who attended one of our events and asked them if they wanted to run for office. The response was extraordinary. More than 7,000 people—from virtually every state—responded.

So we got to work—hosting training sessions to connect them with progressive organizations that would give them the tools they needed to run an effective campaign.

Interestingly, more than 40 percent of the people who raised their hands indicated they wanted to run as Independents rather than Democrats.

We have also endorsed and provided assistance to a number of strong progressive candidates around the country, including Dr. Abdul El-Sayed for Senate and Donavan McKinney for Congress in Michigan, Rebecca Cooke for Congress in Wisconsin, Adelita Grijalva for Congress in Arizona, Robert Peters for Congress in Illinois, and Troy Jackson for governor in Maine.

Perhaps the endorsement that attracted the most attention was for Zohran Mamdani, who was running for mayor of New York City. Mamdani had volunteered for my presidential campaign in 2016 and was a strong progressive, and I was happy to support him when he ran for the New York State Assembly.

Almost no one thought Mamdani had a chance of beating former governor Andrew Cuomo in the Democratic primary. When he began his campaign, he was way, way down in the polls. He was heavily outspent by Cuomo, who had significant support from the billionaire class. But Mamdani's campaign, which focused on making the city affordable for working people, was catching on and he was gaining momentum.

Mamdani wanted my support, and we spoke on the phone a few weeks before the election. I was very impressed. He was giving serious thought to what it would take to run a troubled city like New York, and he was running an extraordinary grassroots campaign involving tens of thousands of volunteers. I decided to support him, as had Alexandria Ocasio-Cortez a few days earlier.

And, to the shock and consternation of the New York establishment, he won.

Mamdani's victory over the entire Democratic machine was a huge step forward for working-class politics not just in New York but throughout the country. His victory gave hope to millions of Americans who learned that you can stand up to corporate greed and the oligarchs, be heavily outspent, and win an important election. Mamdani showed that a progressive economic agenda plus door-to-door campaigning is a winning formula.

6

WHERE DO WE GO FROM HERE?

We are living in unprecedented times. We have to respond in unprecedented ways and with an unprecedented sense of urgency.

Most Americans understand that our current economic and political system is broken—and they want change. Real change. Donald Trump *is* providing change, but it is change based on lies, hatred, divisiveness, self-interest, and policies that benefit the very rich at the expense of everyone else.

Our job, at this critical moment in our history,

is to provide a very different path forward. We must offer an honest explanation to the American people as to how our country got to where it is today. We must expose Trump for the self-serving and authoritarian fraud that he is. We must fight for an agenda that works for the working class of this country. We must mount a massive fifty-state grassroots political organizing campaign that brings Americans together around that agenda and that achieves political power.

None of that is easy, but that's what we've got to do. NOW.

The American People Want Real Change

In a rather extraordinary 2023 poll by the respected Pew Research Center, around six in ten respondents (58 percent) said that life for people like themselves is worse today than it was fifty years ago. I did a questionnaire for people in my own state of Vermont and got a huge response with similar results. Think about that for a minute.

Today, we have drugs and lifesaving medical treatments that didn't exist in the past. We have computers, cell phones, giant flat-screen TVs, hundreds of cable channels, Netflix and Hulu, AI-powered chatbots, robots, Uber, self-driving cars, Spotify, and all kinds of other modern amenities that didn't exist fifty years ago. Yet most people believe that life is worse today than it was back then. In that same poll, only 19 percent of Americans said they are satisfied with the way things are going in the country, while 80 percent are dissatisfied.

Why is that?

Clearly, it has a lot to do with economics. Wages have been stagnant for decades. Some 60 percent of Americans live paycheck to paycheck. We have the highest rates of childhood and senior poverty of almost any major country on Earth. Millions can't find affordable housing. Our educational systems—from childcare to college to trade schools—are inadequate and far too expensive. Our health care system is almost completely broken *and* wildly expensive, with 85 million uninsured or underinsured, and not enough doctors, nurses, dentists, psychologists, or pharmacists.

And parents worry that their kids will be even worse off than they are.

As bad as the economic pain is for working families, it's not just that. The problem goes even deeper. It's our overall quality of life—a sense that things are just not working.

People get in their cars in the morning to drive to work and their blood pressure rises as it takes them an hour to go a few miles because of traffic jams. If you live in a large city and take the subway, it's often an unpleasant experience—dirty, overcrowded, unreliable, and sometimes unsafe. And then you walk to work past people who are sleeping out on the streets, or who are mentally ill and screaming obscenities. And if you're traveling by plane—good luck. Delays. Cancellations. Getting to your destination on time is the rare exception.

Simple tasks become ordeals. Try getting on the phone to dispute a bill with an insurance company or a cable TV company or to make a plane reservation, much less going to the DMV. You're on hold forever, talking to a machine if you get lucky. If you ask your local city council to fix a streetlight, it might be months—or years—before it gets addressed. And what about all the forms you have to fill out when you walk into a doctor's office—if you can find a doctor at all?

And for working-class and low-income people, the challenges are even starker. You are forced to jump through ever more bureaucratic hoops to get access to nutrition assistance, Medicaid, or Social Security, if you qualify at all. If you're living in a poor neighborhood, especially a minority one, try finding a grocery store where you can buy healthy food—or try simply taking a walk at night. I remember speaking to a group of seniors in a Black neighborhood in Baltimore who were afraid to leave their homes in the evening—and it's not just Baltimore. And it's not just Black neighborhoods. The crime problem is real all over the country.

There is also a deep sense that we are losing

touch with what's most important in life, and it is leaving a huge hole in our emotional well-being. Our sense of community is breaking down, and we're seeing huge increases in people who feel lonely and socially isolated. There has been a significant increase in the prevalence of mental illness over the last several decades, suicide rates in the United States have reached a seventy-year high, and youth suicide attempts are rising sharply. In recent years, the number of adolescents reporting feelings of sadness and hopelessness have also risen. When I speak to teachers in Vermont, I'm often told that a good part of their day in school is not teaching their lessons but providing emotional support to kids who are hurting.

At a time when the oligarchs are becoming richer and more powerful and are shaping our future, we live in a world where the adage "The operation was a success, but the patient died" has become a general truth. The system is working successfully for the people who own it, but not so well for the rest of us who are living in it. The rich get richer while ordinary people struggle to survive economically and emotionally.

Now, I am not the only person who understands that reality. Nor are you. Donald Trump gets it as well. That's why he was the "change candidate" in the last election. The only problem is that most of the major changes Trump has implemented are not what he promised his supporters. They are policies that benefit his oligarch friends and are making a bad situation even worse for the American working class.

Trump Lied to Supporters

During his campaign for president, Trump gave long speeches at his rallies. He talked about a lot of things, and, in some cases, he followed through once he was elected. He said he would seal the borders to illegal immigration, and that has largely happened. He said he would end taxes on tips and overtime, and provide tax relief to seniors. And these things are now law.

While Trump carried through on some campaign promises, on the most important economic issues facing working families he did exactly the opposite of what he proposed. In fact, Trump has betrayed millions of his working-class supporters—especially through provisions that were included in his landmark piece of legislation, the "Big Beautiful Bill." Trump has made life a lot harder for the working families of this country.

Let's be clear:

Trump did NOT campaign on giving a trillion dollars in tax breaks to his billionaire friends, or $900 billion in tax breaks to large corporations.

Trump did NOT campaign on making the largest cuts to Medicaid in American history and throwing 15 million low-income and working-class Americans off their health insurance plans.

Trump did NOT campaign on raising health insurance premiums by more than 75 percent, on average, for some 20 million Americans who receive their health insurance from the Affordable Care Act.

Trump did NOT campaign on reducing access to health care for millions of Americans by cutting funding for community health centers, rural hospitals, and nursing homes.

Trump did NOT campaign on taking away free school meals from up to 16 million low-income and working-class kids throughout the country.

Trump did NOT campaign on doubling or, in some cases, tripling monthly student loan payments for millions of Americans who are already drowning in debt.

But it's not just in his "Big Beautiful Bill" where he has betrayed his supporters.

Trump did NOT campaign on shutting down Social Security field offices or making it harder for seniors and the disabled to apply for their Social Security benefits over the phone. He did NOT campaign on firing over 7,000 employees in the Social Security Administration.

Trump did NOT campaign on making it harder for our nation's veterans, those who put their lives on the line defending this country, to receive the health care and other benefits they have earned by proposing to fire 83,000 workers at the Department of Veterans Affairs.

Trump did NOT campaign on a $50-billion-a-year voucher program that will create a two-tier education system in America: private schools for the wealthy and grossly under-resourced public schools for the working-class, poor, and disabled.

Trump did NOT campaign on substantially raising prices for the average working-class family by enacting arbitrary across-the-board tariffs.

Trump did NOT campaign on giving corporate bosses free rein to illegally fire, intimidate, or harass workers who want to form a union by effectively shutting down the National Labor Relations Board (NLRB), the federal agency in charge of holding corporate union busters accountable for breaking the law.

Trump did NOT campaign on eliminating the constitutional right of over a million civil servants, a third of whom are veterans, to collectively bargain for better wages, benefits, and working conditions.

Trump did NOT campaign on appointing more billionaires to his cabinet than any president in American history. Trump has not drained the swamp as he promised to do. Instead, Trump's cabinet epitomizes the swamp.

Rethinking Our Values, Sense of Purpose, and National Priorities

The American people are hurting. They have lost faith in the current economic and political systems, and they believe our country is moving in the wrong direction. If we're going to bring our people together and restore faith in our government and in each other, we need a bold economic and social agenda that speaks to the needs of the long-neglected working class of our country—the people that I grew up with. But we need even more than that.

We need to question the fundamental moral values that underlie the dominant behavior in our society today.

Is it morally acceptable that the top 1 percent

own more wealth than the bottom 93 percent? Are we comfortable with the reality that while billionaires have more money than they could spend in a thousand lifetimes, millions of children in our country go hungry, 800,000 people are homeless, and some 60,000 die unnecessarily each year because they can't afford health care? How much wealth should any one person have? When is enough enough?

As we gather in our churches, synagogues, or mosques, how do we feel about all that? What happened to the Sermon on the Mount, when Christ said, "Do unto others as you would have them do unto you"? Is that just old news—for suckers and "losers"?

Was Christ kidding when he said, "It is easier for a camel to go through the eye of a needle than for someone who is rich to enter the kingdom of God"? Have greed and the worship of the Almighty Dollar become our national religion? Do we now bend the knee before the altars of Wall Street and High Tech?

Do we really believe that "greed is good"? Is life really about the survival of the fittest and every person for himself? Do we think that people who lie, cheat, and steal their way to the top are worthy of our respect, while the kindergarten teacher who spends years caring for our kids for $50,000 a year is a "loser"?

And what are the goals for our nation? What are we striving for in the future?

Should we continue to have the shortest life expectancy of almost any wealthy nation, or should we guarantee health care for all, make prescription drugs affordable, focus on disease prevention, and become an example to the world of what a healthy society looks like?

Do we really need to spend over $1 trillion a year on the military, more than the next ten nations combined, while we have the highest rate of child and senior poverty of almost any major country on Earth? Shouldn't we understand that the children of our country are our most precious resource, and provide them and their parents with the joyful and supportive childhoods they deserve? Shouldn't we show appreciation to the seniors of our country who raised us, built our economy, fought in our wars—and make sure that they have a secure and satisfying retirement?

Should we become more dependent on fossil fuels when carbon emissions are rapidly heating the planet and are creating an existential threat to human life on Earth? Or should we bring the global community together in a massive effort to move our energy systems away from fossil fuels and toward energy efficiency and sustainable energy?

Bottom line: Do we want to remain a nation led by oligarchs, in which the very rich become much richer while tens of millions fall further behind? Or do we want to be a vibrant democracy that leads the world forward into an era of economic well-being for all? That's the fundamental choice we have to make.

Where Do We Go from Here?

The United States is the wealthiest nation in the history of the world. With the proper utilization of AI, robotics, and other new technologies, we will become even wealthier. Given that reality, we now have the opportunity to create the kind of society that has only been dreamed of in the past—a nation in which every man, woman, and child has a decent standard of living. This is not utopian thinking. This is doable, and exactly what we should be fighting for.

If we're going to achieve that goal, here is *some* of what we have to do:

Defend and expand democracy. We are now in a life-and-death struggle to preserve democracy and defeat authoritarianism. The oligarchs like authoritarianism. Without democratic intervention, they can set the rules and do whatever they like to benefit their interests. An authoritarian government makes it easier for them to become even richer and more powerful. Working people need democracy and a responsive government that can advance their interests and put checks on the greed of the oligarchs.

If we are going to successfully defend and strengthen democracy, we must put an end to our corrupt campaign finance system, in which elected officials are beholden to wealthy campaign contributors rather than to ordinary citizens.

We will never have a government that represents the needs of working families so long as billionaires can buy elections. We must overturn the disastrous *Citizens United* Supreme Court decision and abolish super PACs. Democracy is about one person, one vote, not the rich and powerful dominating the political process. We must become a nation where any American can run for office without having to beg the rich for donations.

We must also guarantee that every citizen in our country over eighteen years old is *automatically* registered to vote. No more discriminatory practices of purging voters of color, young people, and low-income Americans from the voting rolls.

We need to end the absurd and extreme gerrymandering that is taking place and has been exacerbated by Republican anti-democratic initiatives around the country. Election districts should reflect a given geographical area, not a space weirdly carved up so that the dominant party can increase its representation.

And, very importantly, we need to move toward the public funding of elections, something that exists in many countries around the world.

We must also take a hard look at the need for electoral college reform. It is impossible to defend a situation in which a presidential candidate wins the popular vote but does not take office.

While we fight for a vibrant democracy, we must also work to create an economy that works for all, not just the few. What follows are a few ideas about how to do this.

Raise new revenue by making the wealthy and large corporations pay their fair share of taxes. In the United States today, we have a tax system that is grossly unfair. It is not acceptable that many billionaires pay an effective tax rate that is lower than what truck drivers or nurses pay. We need a fair and progressive tax system that demands that the wealthiest people in our country finally start paying their fair share of taxes. That includes the enactment of a tax on the extreme wealth of the top 1 percent. Yes. I believe that no one should possess more than a billion dollars in wealth.

Cut military spending. At a time when the Department of Defense is unable to complete an independent audit, and when most observers acknowledge that there is massive waste and fraud in the Pentagon, we should not be spending over $1 trillion a year on our military—including a $150 billion increase in defense spending in 2025 alone, an all-time record.

This bloated military budget is more than the next ten nations, combined, spend for defense. We can make significant cuts in military spending, retain the strong defense that we need, and transfer tens of billions into social needs.

Make certain that the working class benefits from new technology. The technological revolution that is now taking place through AI and robotics will radically transform our economy and our entire society. It is absolutely imperative that the benefits of that revolution flow to all people, not just the corporate world and the high-tech developers of those technologies. AI and robotics cannot simply be another means by which the rich become richer while working-class people lose out.

As the new technologies increase worker productivity, we need to reduce the workweek to thirty-two hours, with no loss in pay. This is a demand that the UAW and other unions are already raising in their contract negotiations. Further, we need to make sure workers receive a fair share of the profits that corporations make from new technology. We should also impose a tax on robotics and AI, and use that revenue to benefit workers who have been negatively impacted by automation.

Guarantee basic human needs. In the richest country on Earth, every American should be entitled to the fulfillment of basic human needs. Wow! That sounds like a radical idea. Maybe. But not as radical as allowing Elon Musk to own more wealth than the bottom half of American households. Not as radical as allowing millionaires and billionaires to avoid paying over $150 billion a year in taxes that they legally owe. Not as radical as allowing oligarchs to stash trillions in secret offshore tax accounts. Not as radical as allowing 60,000 Americans a year to die unnecessarily because they can't afford health care. Yes. In the United States we can afford to provide quality health care, education, nutrition, housing, and retirement security to all—as human rights. And, by the way, a number of countries are far ahead of us in moving in that direction.

What are some of the policy ideas that will provide a secure future for all Americans?

Enact Medicare for All. The United States today is the only major country on Earth not to guarantee health care for all people. Despite spending almost twice as much per capita on health care as the people of any other nation, some 85 million Americans are uninsured or underinsured, half a million go bankrupt every year due to medically related debt, and we have one of the lowest life expectancies of any wealthy nation. One out of four patients are unable to afford the medicine their doctors prescribe because we pay, by far, the highest prices in the world for prescription drugs.

The function of a rational health care system is not to make insurance companies and drug companies tens of billions a year in profits. It's to provide quality care for all and focus on disease prevention. Our current "system" is not only dysfunctional, it is enormously complicated and bureaucratic. We waste huge amounts of money every year in administering a profit-driven system with dozens of insurance companies and hundreds of different policies. The non-partisan Congressional Budget Office (CBO) has estimated that Medicare for All will save the American people $650 billion a year and provide high-quality health care to every man, woman, and child in our country. We can also cut the cost of prescription drugs in half by demanding that pharmaceutical companies not charge us more than they do in Europe or Canada.

Provide quality education for all. The United States used to be the best-educated nation on Earth. Not anymore. In a highly competitive global economy, we have fallen far behind other countries in terms of the percentage of our people with a higher education and how well our kids do on international exams. Today our childcare system is broken, public education is under siege, and higher education is extremely expensive. That has got to change. We must guarantee that every family in America can obtain high-quality childcare for their kids, regardless of income. We must make public colleges and universities tuition-free and cancel student debt. We must provide decent salaries to our public school teachers. We must substantially expand apprenticeship programs and trade schools so that young people can get the training they need to help us rebuild our crumbling infrastructure and move us to sustainable energy.

Make housing affordable. At a time when nearly 800,000 Americans are homeless and over 20 million families are paying at least 50 percent of their limited income on housing, we must expand the National Housing Trust Fund to build at least 4 million more units of low-income and affordable housing, cap the price of rent, end rampant gentrification of neighborhoods, and stop Wall Street speculators from ripping off tenants and flipping homes. It is beyond absurd that young people today are finding it harder to buy their own home than their parents did.

Improve wages and benefits for American workers. Wages and benefits for workers in our country have been stagnant over the last fifty years. Despite working long hours, too many Americans are unable to afford the basic necessities of life. We need a concrete set of policies to improve the standard of living of the average American worker. What follows is some of what we have to do.

Pass the PRO Act. Support for the trade union movement in this country is higher now than it has been in decades. Millions of workers would like to join a union if they could. Too often, however, they are denied that right because of illegal corporate union-busting behavior. The Protecting the Right to Organize (PRO) Act provides severe penalties against businesses that break the law, and makes it easier for workers to form unions and collectively bargain for better wages, benefits, and working conditions.

Raise the minimum wage to a living wage. It is a national embarrassment that the federal minimum wage of $7.25 an hour has not been raised in more than sixteen years, and that nearly 40 million workers make less than $17.00 an hour. In the year 2025, a job should take you out of poverty, not keep you in it. We must raise the minimum wage to at least $17.00 an hour.

Guarantee paid family and medical leave. We must join every other major country on Earth and guarantee paid family and medical leave and paid sick days to workers. Family members should be able to care for a loved one who is sick without having to worry about missing a paycheck. At a minimum, every worker in America must be guaranteed at least twelve weeks of paid family and medical leave, and at least seven paid sick days a year.

Expand Social Security. In the richest country in the history of the world, nearly 22 percent of seniors are trying to survive on $15,000 or less, while half are living on an income of less than $30,000 a year. This is a disgrace. We must substantially increase Social Security benefits so that all seniors can retire with dignity. Legislation I have introduced does that by lifting the cap on taxable income that allows billionaires to pay the same amount of money into Social Security as someone who makes $176,100 a year.

Bring back defined benefit pensions. At a time when about half of older workers have no retirement savings and no idea how they will ever be able to retire with any shred of dignity, we must bring back defined benefit pension plans that guarantee income in retirement. Workers should have the same type of pension plans that members of Congress have, which guarantee a monthly income in retirement.

Encourage employee ownership. There are millions of workers in this country who are tired of being cogs in a machine, with no power over how they do their jobs and how they spend forty or more hours a week of their lives. The result: In Vermont and around the country we have seen a growth in worker-owned and -controlled companies. Studies show that these companies have greater worker satisfaction, less absenteeism, and higher productivity levels. Legislation that I have introduced would provide financial support for workers who want to move to worker-owned companies.

The Political Revolution

Most Americans know that our political system is broken and our economy is rigged. No question: We must fight to reform these things. But we need to begin by doing something even more important. We must reclaim American democracy from the ground up. We must activate millions of people in the political process in a way that has never occurred before. We must wage a political revolution.

It has been said many times, but given the dangerous reality of today, it bears repeating: *Democracy is not a spectator sport*. It's not a football game. It's not a movie. It's not a concert. It's a living process that does not work unless you—yes *you*—are involved. Nobody knows what you want or what you need better than you. Nobody knows what's on your mind better than you. Now, especially now, you cannot sit back and allow the oligarchs and their paid representatives—in government, in the corporate world, in the media—to determine your future for you. No more moaning and groaning. You must be involved.

So. What the hell does that mean? Good question.

Being involved politically can mean many things. It can mean, of course, running for office and serving in an elected position. The truth is that we desperately need to elect dedicated progressive officials at the local, state, and national levels. It is extremely distressing to see, all across the country, that there is often very little competition for seats on the city council, school board, county board, state legislature, and other local offices. These positions are all important and, with a bit of imagination, can become even more important. As someone who served as mayor of a small city for eight years, I can tell you that there is an enormous amount of satisfaction and joy in being able to bring people together at the local level—and delivering for them.

Right now, in partnership with other progressive

organizations, my campaign is in the process of mentoring thousands of people, in almost every state in the country, on how to run for office. So far, approximately 7,000 people have raised their hands to run. Given the widespread concern about the state of the Democratic Party, nearly half of them are running as Independents. We are making good progress in getting candidates to run, but much more needs to be done. We need you.

If running for office is not your thing, there are a lot of other ways that you can be involved in the political process. No candidate wins an election by himself or herself. Campaigns are very much a team effort, and every candidate needs volunteers and, depending on the size of the campaign, paid staff. As someone who has participated in many campaigns, let me tell you something that you may not know. Campaigns can be a lot of fun. You get a chance to work with a lot of people that you'll like. I can't tell you how many couples I've spoken to who met each other on the campaign trail, or activists who have developed lasting friendships.

Further, depending upon what your role is, you may have the opportunity to get outside your comfort zone and interact with folks whose world may be a little different than yours. And that's a good thing.

But let's be clear. Running for office or being involved in a campaign are not the only ways that one can be politically active. Not by a long shot. There are lots of ways to stand up and fight for justice.

It goes without saying that the internet has had a profound impact on modern society. Some of it has been good, some of it not so good. What Trump and his supporters have understood, far more than progressives, is that constant communication is a key to political success—and that, significantly, the internet is the world in which to do it. For better or worse, most people, including the vast majority of young people, no longer get their news or political information from the mainstream media. They get it from podcasts and social media.

One of the positive aspects of the internet is that you can communicate with many people—in your community, in your country, throughout the world—for a minimum amount of money. And you can do it in any way that you feel comfortable—and on any subject. It doesn't have to be just "political." You can talk about economics, health care, education, the environment—anything you want, in any way you want. You can make it personal, you can be "academic"—whatever. The point is that we need to get analyses and visions out there from a different perspective than what the Establishment world and right-wing propagandists show us. We need your help in truth telling and spreading the word. Let's do it.

Several years ago, my campaign started an organization that helps workers organize unions. This work turned into the Emergency Workplace Organizing Committee (EWOC), which trains workers on union organizing. If you've ever been frustrated with what's going on at your workplace, and you want better wages, working conditions, and benefits, now is a good time to do something about it. Join EWOC.

All across the country, ordinary people are now organizing rallies, protests, sit-ins, town halls, and canvasses to stand up to the abuses of the Trump administration. My campaign has trained organizers in nearly two dozen states and hired full-time organizers in several key states. But we're not alone. 50501, Indivisible, and other similar organizations have chapters in nearly every state that hold members of Congress and the Trump administration accountable. Find a local chapter and start organizing.

You can also find specific state and local fights to get involved in. For example, earlier this year, Arizona became the first state to pass a resolution getting Big Money out of Democratic primaries. North Carolina has since followed suit, and other states have efforts underway. This would not have happened without a concerted organizing effort from local activists. From climate change, housing, education, wages, control of our politics, and horrific wars, there is no shortage of local and issue-based campaigns that need your support.

As chairman and ranking member of the U.S. Senate Committee on Health, Education, Labor and Pensions (HELP), I've had the opportunity to meet extraordinary and courageous people from all walks of life and in every part of our country. I always leave those meetings not only inspired but also with the awareness of how much more needs to be done. They need your help.

I've talked to doctors who are sick and tired of being told by insurance companies and corporate boards how to treat their patients. They want quality care for all, not huge profits for drug companies and insurance companies. Join these doctors as they fight for Medicare for All.

I've worked with nurses who came to my office in tears because, as a result of understaffing, they were unable to provide the care their patients required. Some of these nurses actually went out on long strikes so that they could get the staffing levels they needed to do their jobs well. Join these nurses as they fight for quality health care.

I've talked to teachers who, under enormously stressful conditions, are devoting their lives to the well-being of their students, many of whom are from families struggling economically. See what role you can play in working with our teachers and administrators to help create the best public educational system in the world.

I've supported striking workers in every part of this country who have shown enormous courage in standing up to the greed of their corporate bosses. Going out on strike is not easy for workers or their families. Think about joining them on the picket line, or in any other way you can be supportive.

Let me conclude by saying this: Fighting for a vibrant democracy and for economic, racial, social, and environmental justice is not just the right thing to do. This is a fight that most Americans want us to wage—and to win. Despite what Establishment politicians and the corporate media may tell you, the American people do not want to live in an oligarchic society; they do not want to live under authoritarianism; and they do not want to see the billionaire class continue their vicious war against working families.

Yes, I know. The oligarchs have unlimited amounts of money and extraordinary power. They own the media. They control our government and probably own the place where you work.

But this I also know: If we don't let Trump and his fellow billionaires divide us up based on the color of our skin, where we were born, our religion, or our sexual orientation, we can beat the oligarchs and create a much better world. Not just for ourselves, but for our kids and future generations.

Let us stand together and go forward.

Solidarity forever.